How to – Freelance Tips, Tricks and Advice

A small guide to successful freelancing

CONTENTS

INTRODUCTION

Hi and welcome to "How to Freelance: Tips, Tricks and Advice". Inside these pages you will find information regarding techniques and processes that you can use to become a better freelancer.

I personally work in the video game industry, as a Character Artist, and freelance myself to various developments studios working on a range of titles ranging from AAA developers to small indie companies, the likelihood is if you are a video gamer you have probably played a game I have contributed to.

I have had a great deal of success in my field and have decided to share some of the experience within this book. You don't have to be a video game artist to benefit from the advice within these pages. The tips are transferable to different fields within the freelance environment, so if you're a freelance photographer, painter or jewelry crafter then these tips should help you in the same way they do me.

I've tried to separate my advice into several different topics so they're easier to digest. Some bits of advice might be tougher to implement than others given your chosen freelance field but I have found at least a degree of success or usefulness with each.

Anyway I hope something here proves useful and makes your life that little bit easier.

LIFESTYLE

Freelancing is a very tempting lifestyle for people to want to pursue, many believe that working from home and to their own schedule will make life and work easier and more enjoyable, that is definitely not the case. Working from home can definitely be more enjoyable but that it no way means it is any easier.

Personal discipline is a large part of being a successful freelancer, that discipline is needed in your everyday lifestyle as well as the projects you work on. Unfortunately, it's not as simple as ditching your typical 9-5 job, the freelance work environment can be a huge shock to the system both physically and mentally.

The upcoming lifestyle advice and tips help me to maintain focus and ultimately a stable freelancing career.

GET A GOOD NGHTS SLEEP AND HAVE A REGULAR SLEEP PATTERN

This may seem easy and self-explanatory but you would probably be surprised at how easy it is to derail your sleep pattern and railroad your efficiency when freelancing.

There are loads of things that help you maintain a good sleeping cycle, some of which are explained in other points, however the best thing you can do is get yourself into a pattern and be disciplined with it.

Setting an alarm is a good idea or do what I do and set many alarms one after the other, I also find having a shower when I wake up helps to set me on the right path for the day. Another thing is to try your best to avoid any long 'naps' as these greatly disturb your sleeping pattern as well as your energy levels which in-turn will have a knock on disturbance to your efficiency. Naps are not all bad, sometimes when feeling drowsy a strict 10-minute power nap can really help energize you for hours to come, however you have to be extremely disciplined when doing this as napping to frequently can have an adverse effect.

HAVE A HEALTHY DIET

This is probably the hardest thing for a lot of people, even me, and it can have one of the largest detrimental effects on things such as an effective sleep cycle and general wellbeing.

One thing that really helped me was having a regular breakfast. Having something to eat once you wake up can help kick your body into gear. It used to be really tempting for me to skip breakfast and have that extra time sleeping in, however this was counter-intuitive as it meant I was feeling tired and drowsy not to long into the day as my body had nothing in it to work with.

So waking up on time and having a good breakfast can not only make you feel better it can also help regulate your sleeping pattern.

If you drink a lot of sugary drinks such as energy drinks or eat a lot of junk foods you'll initially find, like I did, that you can stay focused for a small amount longer, however after repeated intake of such products you'll eventually get tired and fatigued quicker and more often.

I'm not going to describe or recommend a diet plan as I don't really have any experience with one that has worked for me, only you can decide and initiate that. I will say that drinking a lot of water is a good thing that has helped me a great deal in avoiding gassy/sugary drinks which in turn has helped with my overall general wellbeing.

Again all of this can require a lot of discipline, a consistent trait that you need to implement as a freelancer, but exercising that discipline when it comes to such things as your health is just as important as doing it with your work.

WORK IN A WELL LIT AREA

This might depend on your chosen field but as a digital artist I cannot emphasize how important it is to be able to control your own lighting.

I used to work in a large studio where the lighting was a blanket solution for the entire development floor and this can contribute largely to feeling tired before you should. If you're working in front of a monitor for long periods of time, I'd recommend a window with a lot of natural light as well as a lamp for when it starts to get dark. It's no scientific secret that working in a dark environment can contribute to tiredness, there is also a lot of health benefits associated with natural light so be sure not to confine yourself to a work cave and make sure you have some exposure to the outside world.

Switching up your entire work environment can also help you stay engaged. I spend way too much time sat in my office in front of my computer which over time can become physically draining in itself. When I become conscious of this I'll get up and switch to working on my laptop in a different area of the house or outside, I'll occasionally leave the house all together and do some work at my local café.

DO NOT WORK IN YOUR BEDROOM

I initially had my freelance set-up in my bedroom before moving it to my office, this is a huge mistake, especially if you work long hours, and like me, love your sleep time.

By working in your bedroom you're basically tempting fate and running the risk of regularly feeling drowsy. It can become very easy to think 'maybe I could have a 20-minute nap', all of a sudden those 20 minutes have become 6 hours and you've lost most of your working day and messed up your sleeping pattern.

It can also make waking up for work a problem as your workstation/facilities are so close, by moving your work life outside of your bedroom you at least ensure that you have to get out of bed which is typically the thing a lot of people struggle with.

Another tip for this which also ties into defining your sleep pattern is having your wake up alarm out of reach. As an example most people will have their alarm set and on their bedside table, instead of doing this put your alarm beyond your reach or on the other side of the room requiring you to get out of bed to disable it, this should hopefully help in overcoming one of the mornings toughest obstacles.

WORK SOMEWHERE WITH NO DISTRACTIONS

If you have a large family or a few needy pets then it can potentially make life a little more difficult as every time you're pulled away from your work it then requires a large deal of effort to get back doing it, especially so if you're working on something that you're not particularly invested in.

Having an office or area you can retreat to is often the easiest, however sometimes, you just can't escape things that happen around you in a home environment. Like I suggested in an earlier tip you could get up and remove yourself to a completely different environment such as a café if that's an option.

One thing I did was to instill a behavior in those around me at home. As I still worked to a schedule I basically told those around me to treat my work times as if I was out at a traditional job, so unless it cannot be avoided they're not to bother me during my working hours. This can be easier said than done, especially if there are children, pets or any other dependent thrown into the mix.

SURROUND YOURSELF WITH INSPIRATION

This can present itself in many forms. I personally have figurines, movie and car posters as well as 'art of' books all in my office.

Surrounding yourself with interesting and inspirational items can help you maintain motivation as well as helping generate ideas for whatever it is you're working on. It can also be a great form of focus on a goal, maybe the car poster on the wall is something you're saving up for or the Transformers film poster keeps the dream of working on those movies alive.

For me in my field it's a great source of idea generation. If I have an artistic block, I can take a second to flick through an inspirational 'art of' with the aim of invigorating my imagination. If you're a writer then having some of your most favorite books within reach and reading some could help overcome writers block, painters having prints on the wall from some artists that inspire you can help keep you driven.

LIMIT SOCIAL MEDIA USAGE

If your business relies heavily on social media, then this might not be an option. Some of my advertisement is done through social media, however when doing work, I relegate my social media use to during break times.

In essence thinking like you're working a regular 9-5 job comes in handy here as most places of work limit such use of social media and potentially ban the use of mobile phones, you obviously don't need to be anywhere as strict but a bit of discipline and focus when it comes to working is a very big help indeed.

Something that has worked for a fellow freelancer within my circle is disabling internet access altogether during certain times of the day, this way he is far less tempted to see what's on Facebook or go on a web surfing binge.

BE INTERESTED IN WHAT YOU DO

This goes without saying, you have to have an interest in your work to be able to happily enjoy the freelance life. I see a lot freelance individuals who are not successful and don't understand why, typically it's because they're not truly interested in their field and this comes across in their work portfolio and how frequently they produce work.

Not every client you work for is going to give you work that you're emotionally invested in either, so getting some enjoyment out of what you do is a necessity.

A lucky few will be able to pick and choose the work they do always enabling them to work on something they enjoy, if you fall outside that minority then it's a good idea to make time to work on things you do enjoy outside of client work, this will help keep you focused and motivated on the jobs which are maybe not so interesting.

LISTEN TO MUSIC OR SOMETHING IN THE BACKGROUND

This doesn't work for everyone, there is a small amount of people that enjoy working in pure silence, even I do from time to time but most of the time some form of background noise in a good idea.

You'll have your own things of interest that keep you mentally engaged, I personally listen to music or have video's on in the backdrop, for me it acts as a form of non-interactive company, something I don't have to concentrate on but makes me feel a lot less isolated when working. iTunes and Spotify are great sources of music whereas YouTube, Netflix, Twith.tv etc... are great sources of video and entertainment.

I regularly find that having tutorials for my work discipline playing in the background can help in a number of ways. It helps create a better working atmosphere that's less isolating but I also find I can passively take in some of the information that's being relayed. An example would be doing a painting whilst having a Bob Ross episode on in the backdrop or writing whilst listening to an audiobook from the same genre you're creating.

ALWAYS HAVE SOMETHING TO WORK ON

This is one way to effectively use your downtime or when you're pushing through a work drought. There are many reasons why you would want to always be doing something even when you're not doing client work.

Your personal work can still make you an income (more on that later), it also enables you to try things which you otherwise wouldn't be able to when working to a specific brief set by the client. You can learn new techniques and new pieces of software, it's also a fantastic time to do something that keeps your portfolio up to date as well as maintaining your social media presence when you post updates.

Alternatively, to working on something related to your main discipline you can have a hobby partially or entirely unrelated. Participating in different activities is a great way to gain experience which can help your main focus develop. As an example I like to draw and paint during my downtime, when I do this I gather reference and educate myself on the subject I am creating, this can sometimes lead me down paths I otherwise wouldn't wonder when doing my freelance work, so in turn it could help me inform or inspire the work I create for my clients.

KEEP UP TO DATE

A brilliant trait of any successful freelancer is a hunger to do better and develop their own skillset.

A lot of people who attempt to develop a freelance career generally lack the skills or experience to succeed in the first place, in fact it's generally a good idea that you have some good experiences within your field before taking the leap to become freelance. That said some of the most experienced people I've worked with lack up to date skills so much so that if they were suddenly made redundant or lost their job they would have a great deal of trouble competing against fresher less experienced people.

It's good to stay up to date in your field for many reasons, one of which is if you did lose your job then you're still relevant and competitive, the same goes for freelancers. Being freelance, in most cases, is a more isolated path and doesn't include that competitive drive you have against co-workers in a traditional job, so it's imperative to develop this behavior when working alone.

I'm always working on something to test new techniques and keep my skills well-oiled so that people can see that I'm always working but also so that clients can see I can still contribute to their next project.

If you have a list of outdated skills on your CV it can be an immediate turn off, it's also a bad idea to list skills which you don't really have a good idea about or how to execute them in practice as this could be exposed when on the job which won't be good for future relationships as you're potentially costing your client additional money.

So to recap, it's a good skill to be hungry for personal development and staying up to date and competitive.

EXERCISE REGULARLY

A lot of today's creative freelance work requires a lot of time sitting at a desk whether it be typing your own novel, digital painting in Photoshop or creating a website.

Sitting at a desk for long periods of time generally isn't good for your back, posture and circulation, plus it can add to the onset of fatigue as well as many other ailments. It's worth getting up every hour or so and stretching or having a little walk around the room.

Whenever I start to feel drowsy or feeling a bit of an ache I'll get up and go outside into my garden and have a little walk around and stretch, most of the time this makes me feel a lot fresher and helps me maintain a good work efficiency. If that still doesn't eliminate the issues I will either, make myself a cup of coffee or splash some cold water on my face to help kick me back into gear.

There are many ways to stave off the effects of work fatigue but be sure you don't over work yourself.

TAKE REGULAR WORK BREAKS

This could potentially tie in with regular exercise, either way sometimes stepping away from your work and looking or concentrating on something else will help your work attention overall in the long run.

When it comes to art this is a regularly used technique, I frequently mix up my work jumping from project to project so that my eyes stay fresh.

When working on something for a prolonged period of time you start to become funneled and will have a harder time recognizing the mistakes you make, I find this to particularly be the case when painting and writing not noticing perspective irregularities or spelling/grammar issues.

So again the simple cure to avoid becoming blinkered is to get up and take a little break, returning to work with a fresher perspective.

BE AWARE OF DOWNTIME AND WORK DROUGHTS

It's been mentioned several times already and it's a worthy point all by itself. The chances are at some point or another you will have no paying work in your schedule, this happens more frequently for some and can vary in its length when it does occur, consider yourself fortunate if you work in a field where your skills are in demand. No matter your success as a freelancer you have to plan for this, both financially and mentally.

You have to be pretty smart with your income, leaving you enough buffer to see you through these potentially stressful times, just because you're not getting paid doesn't mean your bills/expenses halt, so be smart when it comes to dealing with your finances.

If within your means it could be a good idea to employ someone to help you with this, alternatively you could do what many others do before pursuing a freelance career and that's save up a good financial reserve so you have money to fall back on should you need it.

Another, more irregular method is to have a part time job to supplement your freelance lifestyle or maybe even getting a small job during predictable work droughts. This isn't something I would personally employ as I'm conscious of potentially relying on that income to much it would separate me from my freelance career which I enjoy. I mention this as I have friends which employ both of these methods with a good deal of success, one does part-time lecturing at Universities which takes up a couple of hours a week and another does Quality

Assurance testing over the summer months when his schedule is typically less packed.

HAVING A GOAL

As cheesy as it sounds you need to have some sort of goal or several goes to be working towards. We're all motivated by different things so our goals will vary from individual to individual but having a goal however small can help drive us to do well when working.

This goal could be that you want to earn 'X' amount a month, it could be a purchase you're working towards or the aim of working for a specific client, studio or project. I specifically like to work on particular projects that inspire me and feed my creativity. This is a big motivation factor for me, it's another reason to do what I do other than the traditional reasons, in some cases this can be a better motivator than the financial gain itself.

SELF-PROMOTING AND GETTING WORK

It's every freelancers dream to sit back and let the work come to them, the reality is that very few freelancers have this luxury, there is also a great amount of work involved in getting to the level where there is no need to self-promote. It can take people years to successfully develop a self-perpetuating brand that has reliable clients.

Self-promotion should be taken very seriously and a decent amount of effort and in some cases money should be invested into the exposure of your brand. It can be easier to market yourself depending on your chosen discipline, despite that there are some things that no one can afford not to have.

There are plenty of tools available to aid in promoting yourself and gaining access to that next job, the following section is dedicated to some of these methods.

HAVE A WEBSITE

This is basically your store front, your business card, your dating profile… It's effectively a huge part of your freelance identity.

You cannot think you will be a successful freelancer without having a good website to promote yourself and you'd be amazed at how many people try to access a freelance career yet negate this very important tool. Having a website is a great way to gain exposure, it can also be used to gather contact information and generate work leads.

Depending on what you do as a profession your website might be an online store, I even have a store on my website for tutorials and assets despite this not being my main focus.

How to build a good website is a separate book in itself but it goes without saying that it needs to be easy to navigate and readable with the least amount of clicks to reach an intended page. It's got to be up to date, relevant and non-offensive, avoid irregular colour schemes and use a font that is easy to decipher and complements your websites aesthetic.

If you don't feel confident making your own website, then why not hire another freelancer to build it for you? Alternatively, you could use one of the wealth of online hosting companies to help you get started.

Although not essential it's typically a good idea in most fields to have your own domain name as well as a website address that is easy to remember, I know that last one sounds obvious but you would be surprised at how many artists I've come across who cannot remember their own website address.

HAVE AN EMAIL ADDRESS AND CONTACT NUMBER

Everyone should have an email address nowadays, it's advisable that it is a professional sounding one and not an address you made when you were 16.

Your contact number should be something people are guaranteed to get in touch with you on, I typically give people my mobile/cell number as it never leaves my side. Both of these should be visible on your site, preferably on the front page.

They should also be implemented onto every piece of promotional material you generate, of course it might not be a great idea to add your personal mobile/cell number to everything you produce but you could always add a website address or email stamp to images of your work, just be sure they're not to overbearing or distracting away from the content itself.

A point to note, if you have a freelance career which caters to customers internationally be prepared to accept calls at all hours, I've had several calls in the middle of the night of which girlfriend did not appreciate. Most however won't have to worry as email is generally the method most employ when first contacting you.

HAVE A LINKEDIN ACCOUNT

LinkedIn is like an online business card, an open CV, a sort of Facebook site of the business world where you connect with other people within your professional circle. This can be a really good way to connect with recruiters and agencies who frequently post freelance positions and jobs most of which don't mind direct contact via LinkedIn.

Most companies also have their own profiles on LinkedIn which are updated with the latest news on recruitment. You can choose to follow these companies and have the updates published to your own customized LinkedIn feed.

Like Facebook you can also create your own posts and updates. If you're looking for work, it's usually a good idea to post that fact on LinkedIn and if you have a network of recruiters of agencies they will potentially seek you out.

I don't really have a massive LinkedIn network yet I get people contacting me on a regular basis regarding potential jobs, mainly agencies/recruiters but on the odd occasion I get leads direct from the developers/clients themselves.

HAVE A BLOG

A blog is a good way to consistently update people on your development progress and generally keep readers aware that your still active and working.

Most blogging sites have cross site integration allowing you to create an update and propagate that to the rest saving you a great deal of time in the process.

The blog can also be a good advertisement to potential clients, if they see you consistently putting out work and updates it tells them that you're a consistent worker who is engaged and motivated.

Driving traffic to your blog can be tough especially if you work in a pretty niche market, however when used in conjunction with other exposure methods such as Facebook, Instagram and Twitter you can get a healthy flow of people visiting and hopefully engaging with your blog.

Once on your blog you can create a type of 'squeeze' page which will give readers the opportunity to leave their email address so they can receive updates from you in the future.

These email lists can be handy in the future as you can potentially send your followers products or services that you offer.

If you're lucky enough to have a popular blog than you could potentially earn some additional income by advertising products or utilizing affiliate marketing. This is a bit of a minefield topic which requires a ton of research typically with the need for some financial and time investment.

HAVE A SOCIAL MEDIA PRESSENCE

Having a blog and LinkedIn page tie in with this but it's also worth mentioning the other avenues available such as Facebook, Twitter, Instagram, Pinterest and YouTube, to name but a few. Blanket each of these networks and develop an audience on each, a lot will probably crossover but updating each frequently will gain the attention of many new sets of eyes over time.

Some sites have methods of promoting your material, for example Facebook lets you pay money to boost your posts to a specific audience, this can prove really useful when trying to attain new followers or if you have a product which you want to get in front of people.

A lot of time can be invested in social media before seeing any actual results to your business so it's worth researching its viability and reach. Some people find great success when utilizing the social media platform to promote their products. In some cases, they invest a proportionally small amount of time developing a product/service and a large amount in getting it to propagate and eventually sell through the social media platform.

Again this is a massive topic in of itself with an entire libraries worth of content to get through, just be aware that it could be a potential avenue for developing your freelance proposition.

ADVERTISE YOURSELF VIA POPULAR SITES

Each field has their own go to sites where people congregate to gather and discuss their disciplines. Many of these sites will have sections or job boards where they will allow you to create a thread advertising your services. When making a thread to advertise yourself as a freelancer, be sure it has a catching but professional title, this can represent itself differently depending on your career path but making it short and specific is usually a good idea. Within the thread itself you're aiming to get as much information across as efficiently as possible, good pictures of your work can do a lot better in conveying your skillset then your words can, especially if you work within a creative industry.

Be sure that you post your contact details so people can get in touch. I'd also advise to refrain from stating your rates unless it's typical of your line of work, doing so can potentially put people off before they've even had a chance to talk to you, which is wasted potential work and the loss of a future contact or professional relationship.

Be sure to frequently update and bump the thread, either after a few days of it lying dormant or when you're again available to do work. Check back often to see if anyone has posted within your thread or used the forums private message facility to contact you directly regarding work. Finally, always reply to each question or query as promptly as possible and as professionally as you can.

FREQUENT FORUMS AND POST WORK PROGRESS

Some disciplines have more facilities to interact with the communities which make up your field. It's a good idea to expose yourself to as many of these communities and contribute as much as possible. Participating on forums isn't incredibly difficult but can sometimes be time consuming depending on how many you frequent and how regularly you choose post.

I particularly enjoy posting my personal work on such sites to try and engage with fellow members of the community. By posting my works in progress I can actively seek feedback from other forum goers on my work, some of which can be really useful when it comes to personal development, likewise I'll do the same for other members offering my critiques and advice where applicable. If you do a decent job at this you could become a valued member of that online community, the world is a small place and it can pay dividends, as eventually other members might come to you with potential work or opportunities.

Remember it's incredibly likely that many of your clients will also frequent such communities to scout for potential talent, so it's always a good idea to remain polite and conduct yourself in a professional manner.

ADVERTISE ON FREELANCER SITES LIKE ODESK AND ELANCE

There are several dedicated freelance sites which sole job is finding freelancers work. These sites work in a variety of ways, typically you advertise yourself and people pick and choose the best freelancer for the job, contacting them directly and working out a deal. Alternatively, some potential clients post their brief and budget enabling the freelancer to contact them and again arrange some sort of agreement.

These sites are pretty competitive and you really have to differentiate yourself from the wealth of other people looking for work, also be careful of who you want to work with and do some research on your client prior to signing any contract, luckily these sites tend to make this relatively easy utilizing a rating and recommendation system.

I personally find these websites cater to high frequency tasks with low rates as opposed to larger projects with longer timeframes, for some this is an ideal platform where they generate a majority of their income, however for certain fields of work, including mine, these sites have little to offer. Either way it's worth having a look as it could be exactly what you're after.

ATTEND EVENTS AND MEET UPS

As well as social networking via digital platforms you can do the traditional thing and physically socialize at events.

Attending events is a good way to build your contact library and promote yourself as a brand. Don't forget your business cards, CV/Resume's and copies of your work/portfolio.

Events can also be a good place to meet your peers or friends from relationships which have been cultivated online, some of my higher quality work leads have developed from such relationships so it's worth investing some energy in trying to make new friends. It's also a good way of getting you outside of the house if you're one of those freelancers who spends most of their waking life at home developing their business.

Most of these events are advertised online via forums or on websites, some you may have to pay or travel a considerable distance for so it's up to you whether you deem them worth it.

As well as events which aim at socialization there are events which actually deal with recruitment. Recruitment fairs are typically held by companies or recruitment agencies with the aim of recruiting within a specific field.

In my experience within my discipline a lot aim to hire full-time or part-time on site employee's, however it's a good opportunity to speak directly to the advertisers about their company's recruitment needs and if they cater to freelancers in general. You can always hand over your business card or CV/Resume and plant the seed.

BUSINESS CARDS

You'll need a business card for those events, make sure you get some, make sure they're professional and to the point. Don't use any fancy fonts or outrageous colours, unless these are representative of your business in which case you could probably get away with it, just be sure it's eligible.

The key here in most cases is to play it safe and keep it simple, sharp and professional, be sure your name, professions, email, contact number and web address are clearly displayed and easy to read.

Also if meeting people in person be sure to exchange business cards or gather them where you can to add to your contact list.

CHECK COMPANY SITES DIRECTLY

Possibly one of the easiest methods of attaining work but also one of the most overlooked. Build yourself a list of clients you would like to work for, in my field it would be development studios.

I have all their websites bookmarked for me to frequently visit and check for any new job postings. Often jobs tend to be full time, permanent or in house positions in my field but occasionally there will be remote freelance or contract work available in which instance it's usually a case of applying and interviewing just like any other job. In fact, my most lucrative jobs have come direct from the developer job boards.

Most job boards on sites also allow you to leave your email and subscribe for new job posts and updates so be sure you're doing that as some jobs can go quickly if they're in demand.

Even if there are no jobs posted on the site that currently cater to your needs then there is no harm is sending a quick introductory email to their recruitment or HR department. Again this plants a seed, you can follow this up every so often with more enquiries about the potential for upcoming positions, just don't overdo it and be sure to leave a good amount of time between contact otherwise you come across as being needy which is annoying and is a sure fire way to getting blocked.

CHECK NICHE FORUMS AND WEBSITES

Again like the developer websites check your disciplines forums regularly for new jobs being posted.

Just like you advertise yourself via these forums, companies will also advertise their jobs to. So be sure to bookmark them and check in regularly, if the job is filled, out of date or not specific enough for you, you could always get in touch anyway introducing yourself and gaining a contact for the future.

Some of the major sites relating to your topic might also house the facility for job advertisement. Specifically, in my field the likes of Artstation and Gamasutra have job boards, so be sure to visit your typical resource sites and have a look for any job sections.

CHECK RECRUITMENT SITES, FORUMS AND AGENCIES

Another great way to attain freelance work is via agencies. A lot of companies outsource their recruitment to another company to save themselves time and money, these agencies act as an intermediary between you and your potential employer.

It's common to have to upload a description of yourself and your experience but it's worth doing so. In some cases, certain jobs will only be advertised through the agency and not on the employer website directly so it's a good idea to have a look. Also most agencies allow you to register with them or subscribe for updates, this is a great way to passively look for work, it by no means eliminates the need to source work yourself but occasionally the agency will get in touch with potential offers that fit the bill of what you're looking for.

Just be aware, these agencies don't work for free and their fee has to come from somewhere, yes they do get paid by companies to advertise their jobs but in some cases they will take a chunk of your salary. By this I mean the salary the agency advertises might be lower than dealing with the company direct as you might actually be paying that fee indirectly. Suffice to say agencies are a valuable resource.

CHECK FREELANCING STUDIOS

Many people have made a business of people's freelance business. Most freelancing disciplines have studios set up where they hire freelancers to work on projects that they attain. These studios typically act as the middle man between you and the client similar to that of an agency. They communicate with the client and pass that to you, and from you back to the client.

In many cases these 'studios' don't actually have a physical premises and are just individual freelancers themselves working from home on larger projects that they cannot tackle themselves thus need to outsource some of the work to additional freelancers.

In other cases, there might actually be a physical studio where you journey to work. In these instances, you're brought on for a project but once the project is finished or the contract is over you return to your regular process.

YOUR PROPOSITION

There are some differentiators that can make you stand out among other freelancers.

When communicating with a potential client there are some specifics you'll have to address and there are things you can do which will help sell yourself.

It's a good exercise to imagine that you're an employer yourself, what would you want to look for in an employee? What would make you choose a specific individual over other similarly qualified individuals? By answering questions like this you can come up with some of the answers that will make you a more viable proposition to potential employers.

BE FLEXIBLE AND DIVERSE

This is a pretty broad piece of advice and can manifest itself in many ways. For example, I work with clients all over the world in different time zones, one way I could be flexible is to match my current work schedule to their time zone to create a better communication and feedback loop.

Another might be offering various methods of payment, direct to your bank account, cheque or via an online method such as PayPal. It could also take another form, I typically develop characters for videogames, however I am not averse to doing environment assets or props, in fact I don't limit myself to purely the realm of video games, luckily a lot of the skills I've developed to create video game assets is transferable to film, advertising and online media, so to not bottleneck my income or potential client list I can search for work in those fields as well.

Being diverse and not funneling yourself into an even more specific niche can be huge when it comes to making you stand out from similarly qualified people.

HAVE A DAILY RATE AND A PER PROJECT PRICE

This is a massive topic which would easily spiral into its own little book, I'll try and keep it simple here with a couple of examples. Different clients have varying budgets and because of this are very conscious of the way pricing is presented to them.

Large companies and big contracts tend to, in my experience, prefer a daily rate. This daily rate should factor in several things such as the cost for actual production, your maintenance costs, tax or VAT, health insurance and your general upkeep. Most of this is factored into your salary when working full time in a studio or regular job environment, whereas when you're freelancing you have to pay for everything yourself, most employers understand this and as long as your day rate is reasonable for the quality you're providing, they will have no problem paying it.

On the other hand, smaller clients such as indie studios or individuals might not take to a day rate like a larger establishment would as the time taken to create the product could spiral and end up costing them more then what they have in mind. In these instances, it's good to quote per asset or job. You must tread carefully though and be smart when quoting a single all in figure, you have to factor in the potential for revisions and maintenance of what you produce. For example, if I generate a quote for a character and say that it will take me 2 weeks to complete at a cost of £2,500 then I need to stipulate that I'm willing to make amendments and revisions beyond that but within reason, maybe even limit it to a specific number of revisions.

These are things you want to decipher when generating a contact or agreement. Unfortunately, in some cases what you charge will just be out of someone's budget and they'll be no way they can afford what you quote. This can be for a number of reasons, the most common one I come across is currency conversion, as I live in the UK the Pound (£) is a lot stronger than other currencies so the conversion rates make it so that I unfortunately price myself out of some potential work, typically that from Canada and Australia, hopefully this isn't the case for yourself and you live somewhere which has a less aggressive national currency.

It can be tempting to lower your rate to accommodate lower budgets but this can be harmful as some people might expect you to keep up that rate in the future which might not be viable for your lifestyle long term, so in most instances like this it's best to just let the work go or point the client in the direction of someone else.

CANT DO THE JOB? RECOMMEND SOMEONE ELSE

I've been in the situation several times where I'm just too busy to take on genuine work, in these cases I'll usually recommend someone else who might fit the client's requirements for the job.

This is a really good networking trait which not only develops relationships with your fellow freelancers but can also be good for any future development with that particular client.

Just because you're too busy to contribute to their project now doesn't mean you will not be able to do so in future, so if you recommend someone who does a good job, the client will appreciate it; there is also no harm in returning to that client once you have some time freed up just in case they still require your services.

HAVE REFERENCES AND RECOMMENDATIONS

If you've done a good job and have a decent relationship with a client, then ask them for a recommendation or to be used as a potential reference in future if needed. Recommendations can be added to your CV/Resume and your other promotional assets such as your website/portfolio or LinkedIn.

This is also another reason to be sure you do a good job for each and every client you work for no matter how small the project or pay cheque. The power of a good recommendation is endless likewise the power of a bad review due to poor performance can be devastating.

HIGHLIGHT ACHIEVEMENTS AND AWARDS

Much like recommendations highlight any rewards or achievements you have. For example, I personally entered several modelling competitions which I ranked 1st place in, that's an achievement worth talking about in my line of work.

You can highlight these via your CV/Resume or on your site/portfolio and social media pages. It could also be worth mentioning other types of achievement which fall outside of your field, things such as charity work or fundraising go down really well with any employer as it shows you have some drive and motivation which stands outside that of financial gain.

COMPLETING WORK AND GENERATING INCOME

You can do more than just working on client projects to generate an income, but when working with a client there are somethings you should do to save both your time and theirs as well as protecting you both against potentially bad agreements.

You should always be working and developing your business as a freelancer and if you're good at something then there is generally many ways you can monetize your skillset.

Be sure not to undervalue yourself either, if you're good at something then that skill is worth something to someone. People offering 'exposure' generally have little influence in the first place, so do yourself a favor and charge people a reasonable rate worthy of your time.

Additionally, doing work for free or under valuing yourself can have an adverse effect on your future potential to create a good income, which is a shame as work done for free is usually done under good intention. Working for free essentially decreases your entire fields value and makes it harder for yourself and other freelancers around you doing the same job more difficult to command a sustainable income.

This next section will hopefully highlight some things you can do to generate additional income as well as making your client happy.

DEVELOP PASSIVE INCOME STREAMS

With most freelancers there is a potential for a lot of downtime, especially in a work drought where jobs are less frequent and your income might take a dip.

During this downtime, or times where you have a decreased work output, you can potentially develop a form of passive income. For example, I created 3D Art tutorials which people are willing to pay for, I also wrote a book which generates a small consistent income which can sometimes help me when cash flow is tighter.

Do not underestimate the power of good information, chances are if you're freelancing you have some experience in the field you're working in, this experience can typically be monetized, in fact some freelancers generate a majority of their income of selling such information. There are plenty of websites on the internet which allow you to upload or develop information products for you to sell, the tricky part in advertising such products and generating the views needed to guarantee a good conversion resulting in a form of income.

The great thing about selling your information products is that once you've done the work it is out there generating income with little or no additional maintenance. I personally use several websites to advertise products like tutorials, Gumroad, Selz and Cubebrush are all great websites for creatives to expose their digital products.

MAKE MONEY FROM PERSONAL WORK

If you're working in a creative sector then some of the assets you create in your spare time could be sold, this is a continuation from the last point of passive income, however instead of selling information or experience you're selling something more tangible.

Again to use another personal example, I create 3D art in my personal time to develop my skills, however what I make to improve myself can also be sold. My digital sculpt can be turned into 3D prints, my game assets can be sold to developers via asset stores. Painters can do sell copies/prints of their personal work, Photographers can sell images as stock photography.

DO GUEST LECTURES OR EVENT TALKS

This is a really rewarding method both financially and emotionally. It's a great feeling to add to someone's education and it's relatively common for skilled freelancers to conduct guest lectures or talks at events. Pay for such services vary massively but in most cases companies of institutes are willing to pay a decent hourly rate for you to come and speak to their employee's or students.

I personally conduct several guest lectures a year at different Universities and colleges, I also judge competitions and help with amateur portfolio reviews giving advice to students and upcoming developers. You can get a great buzz from educating others and it can make a real difference to others lives as well as your own.

It goes without saying that this is another great way to expose your brand and has the potential for recurring work in the future as you get the opportunity to develop more professional relationships.

WHEN CORESSPONDING WITH A POTENTIAL CLIENT MENTION MONEY/RATES SOONER

In the start you may get the occasional offer of work or query but after time, after building up contacts a good social presence and after developing good methods of promotion, you will probably receive a large amount of queries.

One way of filtering out the chaff from the solid leads is by mentioning money early. A lot of people want something for free, especially when artists are concerned, they have a notion that creativity comes easily and is done quickly so why not do it cheap or for exposure. Well to maintain a healthy freelance lifestyle you cannot do work for free or exposure, so if you bring up the issue of pay earlier rather than later you can potentially save yourself a lot of correspondence time.

When advertising yourself via whatever method you choose it might be worth stating that you do not work for free or for profit share/royalties, which is another common thing people might offer you as 'payment'. Don't get me wrong, not everyone who asks for free or investment work is sinister or dodgy, it's just in most cases these project/jobs never develop to the point where you get that exposure or profit share. Just be aware that participating in work of that nature is done so at a risk to your earnings.

ALWAYS HAVE A CONTRACT SIGNED BEFORE WORK

I make it a rule to not do any work until a contract is signed by both parties.

In many cases most clients will have their own contract that they issue to freelancers working for them and again most of them are will to make amendments and change the contract if you desire so. For instance, making sure that you stipulate a maximum amount of days needed for feedback, so that you're not waiting for a long time or working on something which is inevitably changed, thus wasting time/money.

In some cases, the client might not have a contract, if that is the case then it is good to have your own to fall back on, likewise it is good to be flexible and amend it if there is anything they wish to add. Typically, most of the amendments are due to the way a thing is worded or regarding feedback and payment information. You'll find a lot of contracts contain a lot of law speak which is usually uninterpretable to the everyday freelancer.

If you find contracts a daunting prospect, then it is generally a good idea to get a lawyer involved to read over the contract to make sure it's safe enough for you to move forward. I've personally not had any issues with employers or contracts, I've had one late payment but luckily I wasn't desperate for the money, however saying this I have had friends run into problems in the past, issues which could have been avoided with a solid contract.

GET AS MUCH INFORMATION UPFRONT

Some clients are purposely vague, but it's preferable if you gather as much information off them upfront when working on their project.

It's generally a good idea to ask as many questions up front to avoid having to ask questions later, this is a good way to avoid working on something which could potentially be going in the wrong direction ultimately requiring revisions or amendments which in turn costs money and time.

In my field I usually ask them for a detailed brief if possible along with any images or examples of how they wish the product to look or feel.

Some client might not have a clue what they actually want, it's then up to you to give them options. Be careful not to give clients like this to many options or too much information as you're likely to overload them and make reaching a definitive direction harder. I usually find projects like this offer more creative freedom and are far more enjoyable, this is one of the reasons I personally got into freelancing within my field.

DON'T BE AFRAID TO ASK QUESTIONS DURING DEVELOPMENT

Just like gathering information upfront is very important, just as important is gathering information during development.

In an ideal world you'd attain a brief and develop a product absolutely ideal for the client without the need for feedback or amendments, unfortunately that is a dream and some issues are only encountered whilst actually working on the project.

It's natural to sometimes feel a bit uneasy having to ask what might seem like a simple question, but it's rarely a bad idea to do so. You have to realize that you're not always going to be dealing with someone who has the same skillset and thought process as yourself, most of my direct contacts on a majority of projects are not even artists like myself, so to avoid undue complication and negate the need for revisions it's a better idea to ask the question rather than get something wrong and pay for it later with your time or their money.

DON'T BE AFRAID TO MAKE SUGGESTIONS

Not every client gives you a specific or stringent brief which cannot be deviated from. Typically, the reason they're relying on you in the first place is because you're experienced in the field and have some success in what you do.

In a vast majority of my client work they generally don't have a fully realized idea and require some input from yourself to create the right product for them. For me this is a great opportunity for me to make my mark on what I'm making and infuse it with of my own ideas.

It doesn't harm your relationship to ask before you make any suggestions or before going ahead and implementing any of your ideas, it's good manners and helps maintain a good working relationship with your client, that and there is always a chance that the client won't want the suggestion or even like what you eventually come up with.

GAIN REFERENCE AND RESEARCH

At the start of any project once you've received a brief from the client it's a good idea to spend a decent amount of time gathering research and reference around the content you're creating. For example, if I'm creating a head for a game character then I'll go looking for images via search engines online for heads which have the look of what the client wants producing, I'd also gather some reference on the smaller details such as skin, wrinkles or even techniques to implement and use during development.

There are plenty of methods to gather reference and conduct research which will differ greatly depending on what field you work in. Once you've gathered your reference or done a chunk of research it's generally a good idea to share what you've got with your client to see if they're along the same lines as you.

UPDATE AND FEEDBACK WITH YOUR CLIENT
FREQUENTLY

There is no better way to sour a client relationship then not feeding back with what you have been working on.

In most cases the client will outline a feedback method for you to follow which will include how frequently you update them and how you do so, whether it be with images or actual work in progress files, however if they don't have a structure in place for you to follow then it's up to you to suggest or create a method that works well for you both. I try and look at these as mini-milestones throughout the project, it's a way of maintaining a good working relationship but also a good method of keeping organized, focused and on track.

Planning out good update and feedback cycles is a great way of maximizing your work time and output, if you do this well you can expose potential gaps or openings in your schedule which could be filled with another small client project or some other form of work to generate income.

IF YOU HAVE TROUBLE DELIVERING THEN LET YOUR CLIENT KNOW

If you're having trouble implementing feedback or if something comes up in your day life that will hinder your ability to make a delivery or finish the work on time, then it's best to let your client know as soon as you know. Most clients are very accommodating and sympathetic to genuine issues which you might encounter.

This is guaranteed to happen at some point during your freelance career, unfortunately there are some things that are beyond our control and it can affect how efficient we are when it comes to our work.

Either way it's generally good manners to let them know of any issues, that way you can both make any arrangements you might need to make to ensure project completion or it gives them a chance to initiate any contingency they have in place for such matters.

TRY YOUR UPMOST NOT TO OVERWORK

It's common to work longer hours on a project then you initially intended to or quoted, it's often the case that I work a couple of hours over my typical work day or even dipping into my weekends to ensure work is of the best quality and completed on time.

Doing the best you can on a project to impress a client or maintain a good relationship will sometimes require additional effort and time however you must be careful. For every hour you work beyond your quoted time you eat into your rates and profit, you also run the risk of hitting a barrier which can cause you to lose interest in what you're working on and potentially cause work fatigue.

Suffice to say overworking can have a detrimental knock on effect, it is also proven that up to a point doing overtime is fine but once beyond a certain amount of time you actually become less effective and run the risks of making mistakes which will eventually need more time and money to rectify.

BE OPEN TO DIFFERENT METHODS OF
COMMUNICATION

Everyone has their preferred method of communication and as a successful freelancer you have to be able to accommodate that.

In a lot of cases it's not feasible to send an email or instant message to discuss a topic, especially so if you're from 2 largely differing time zones. In a large amount of cases a more direct communication approach is needed to save time and avoid any ambiguity which might be present when using a more traditional method. Luckily there are many ways to do this nowadays thanks to the internet.

Skype is probably the most frequent method of communication I utilize as its direct and avoids inflated overseas call rates that phone companies tend to impose. If direct methods are not an option due to unavailability or largely differing time zones then another great way to communicate with a client is via video, just be sure to factor in the time needed to make such a piece of communication into your daily schedule.

DEALING WITH ADMIN

Unfortunately, being a freelancer isn't always working on creative projects or developing your discipline, you have to negotiate the wealth of admin that accompanies it. This can be one of the hardest things to do as a freelancer especially if it's something you're not attuned to doing.

There is the typical day to day admin that your career will need to be well maintained however there are tasks which you'll have to complete far less frequently but carry a lot of importance with them such as a tax return or VAT declaration.

I typically take a day out of monthly schedule to tackle such things as well as allocate a small out of time on a daily basis to make sure I'm up to date with everything.

The next chunk of advice is dedicated to tackling these admin tasks and looking at simple solutions to help people manage the less glamourous side to freelancing.

UTILIZE AN ORGANIZER OR PLANNER

One thing which can be a huge culture shock to people when becoming freelance is the need for organization, you have to have a plan, a roadmap, somewhere to keep your appointments, your contacts and so on.

There are plenty of ways and methods to do this and each individual will have some different process which works for them. For me it was using a piece of software to help me keep organized, in this case it's Microsoft Outlook. Outlook allows me to link several of my personal email addresses which I utilize into one easy, manageable interface as opposed to many different webpages. It also houses a calendar for my day to day planning needs as well as a contact and address book for all my clients, other freelancers and friends.

It can also help in tasking out individual projects, kind of like using post-it notes and placing them around your monitor whereas in this instance it's contained within the software itself. Another plus point is that you can sort all your correspondence with clients easily and have an archive just in case there is anything you need to refer to.

ALWAYS RESPOND TO EMAILS

It can sometimes be a hassle to work through your emails especially if a lot of it is chaff, however make a habit of replying to everyone who makes a query.

At the least it's good manners but it can also make good business sense, for every person who enquires about your services is a future contact or potential job. If you don't end up replying to these people you run the risk of losing work, they could be your boss in the future or have a very lucrative project which you could contribute to, so even if their initial proposition seems lack luster they might have something going forward which may be worth your while, so if you reply to them and do so in a professional manner you're more likely to avoid burning bridges.

KEEP ALL INVOICES AND RECEIPTS, ALSO MAKE PAPER COPIES

In most countries this is a legal necessity as you potentially have to provide these to the relevant tax body to prove your earnings.

It's relatively easy to create your own invoices using readily available software, there is also an abundance of templates online to download, edit and utilize. I keep all my invoices organized on my PC in folders, I also back them up on an additional storage device just for some redundancy. Additionally, make a habit of printing them out and having a hard copy to store and keep for my records.

KEEP TRACK OF INCOME AND OUTGOINGS

Not only is tracking your income and outgoing essential for a successful freelance career it's also a pretty useful life skill in general.

Some successful freelancers hire an accountant to deal with all their expenses and tax related tasks. For some this is a huge time saver and can potentially include a lot of money saving despite having to pay for this facility.

I personally do it myself using various pieces of software and online tools, I find it pretty easy typically due to the infrequency of payments and expenditure, however if your business includes a lot of transactions or you simply don't have the time, patience or experience, it might be worth getting some additional help. For these particular tasks I've created my own Microsoft Excel spreadsheet which calculates my income and expenses I make, I also include tax and VAT values.

If you don't think you can learn to make your own, then you can utilize internet search engines such as Google to gain access to templates which other people have created for you to download and use.

PUT MONEY ASIDE FOR TAX, EXPENSES THE UNEXPECTED AND DROUGHTS

A lot of the prior points help with the unfortunate fact that you have to pay taxes, pay for your expenses such as equipment and save for a potential work drought. Many freelancers simply fail at their career purely because they do not plan for such things.

A little foresight can help avoid any undue stress and create a piece of mind. Whichever method you choose to help save money, just be sure you actually do save money otherwise you could get yourself into a spot of bother which might have an adverse effect on your facility to pursue a freelance career.

When working full time with a consistent income you become accustomed to frequent payments with all the additional costs such as tax and insurance being taken from the source, most of this is automated which makes it really easy, however when working freelance you have to deal with this all yourself manually, so you need to plan and put procedures in place.

I personally separate all my personal and business items, I created another bank account purely to house funds for things such as tax, VAT, health insurance and savings, I than extract a certain percentage of my income and deposit into that account and only utilize it for the things it's intended for.

It's very tempting to spend all the money you get from the work you do but you have to be disciplined, to do so is potentially setting yourself up for trouble or opening yourself up to the possibility of some expensive payouts in the future.

CHECK FOR TAX BREAKS, OFFERS AND INCENTIVES

You might be surprised but in a lot of different countries there are many opportunities to save some money whilst working as a freelancer. For instance, in the UK, if your freelance business is VAT registered you can claim your VAT back on equipment, fuel used for your job and even save money on your utility bills if you work from home.

It's worth doing a large amount of research into the different ways you can save money when running your own business.

CONCLUSION

So that's all the tips I've got for you at the moment. I hope someone out there finds some of the information provided useful or enlightening. I also hope I didn't put anyone off following their freelance dream.

Make no mistake freelancing can be a hard and brutal career with the need for a lot of time, energy and patience, however it can also be immensely rewarding and liberating.

With some preparation, consideration and hard work you can make a freelance career generate a great income and have a lot of fun whilst doing it, now that I'm freelancing successfully I'd find it very hard to return to a regular job.

If you've found anything within these pages useful then I'd encourage you to share this information with your friends and direct the book their way, also if at all possible leave a review on the site you got the book from.

With that said I'd like to thank you for reading my small book and I hope you have many successful endeavors with your freelance adventures.

Thanks again

Lance Wilkinson

P.S If you're interested in my background or career or want to see what type of content I produce then by all means please visit my personal sites over at

https://lancewilkinson.weebly.com

https://gumroad.com/optinium

https://www.facebook.com/theartoflancewilkinson

If you want updates on what I'm up to then you can sign up to my follow page via the following link

https://gumroad.com/optinium/follow